Animal Babies

W9-CNA-142

Insects

Rod Theodorou

Heinemann Library
Des Plaines, Illinois

Customer Service 1-888-454-2279

Text designed by Celia Floyd
Illustrations by Alan Fraser
Printed in Hong Kong/China

04 03 02 01 00
10 9 8 7 6 5 4 3 2 1

The Library of Congress has cataloged the hardcover version of this book as follows:
Library of Congress Cataloging-in-Publication Data
Theodorou, Rod.
     Insects / Rod Theodorou.
        p. cm. – (Animal babies)
     Includes bibliographical references and index.
     Summary: Introduces the birth, development, care, feeding, and
characteristics of insect young.
     ISBN 1-57572-880-X (lib. bdg.)
     1. Insects—Infancy—Juvenile literature. 2. Parental behavior in
animals—Juvenile literature. [1. Insects. 2. Animals—Infancy.
3. Parental behavior in animals.] I. Title. II. Series: Animal
babies (Des Plaines, Ill.)
     QL495.5.T48 1999
     595.713'9—dc21   99-18052
                                                                        CIP
Paperback ISBN 1-57572-543-6

Acknowledgments
The Publishers would like to thank the following for permission to reproduce photographs:
BBC/Hans Christoph Kappel, p. 6; Pete Oxford, p. 9; Bruce Coleman/Kim Taylor, p. 8; Felix Labhardt, p. 25; Frank Lane/ E. & D. Hosking, p. 8; B. Borrell, p. 13; NHPA/Martin Harvey, p. 7; Anthony Bannister, p. 22 Stephen Dalton, pp. 17, 18, 24; Oxford Scientific Films/Phil Devries, p. 5; Tim Shepherd, p. 10; Scott Camazine, p. 11; Avril Ramage, p. 12; J.H. Robinson, p. 15; K. G. Vock, p. 16; G. I. Bernard, p. 19; P. & W. Ward, pp. 20, 21; Neil Bromhall, p. 23; Tony Stone/Art Wolfe, p. 14.

Cover photo: Oxford Scientific Films/Michael Fogden

Some words in this book appear in bold, **like this.** You can find out what they mean by looking in the glossary.

Contents

Introduction 4

What Is an Insect? 6

Laying Eggs................................8

Taking Care of the Eggs 10

Hatching Eggs............................12

Finding Food 14

Taking Care of Baby 16

Staying Hidden..........................18

Staying Safe..............................20

Amazing Changes........................22

Splitting Skins 24

Growing Up..............................26

Insects and Other Animals..............28

Glossary 30

More Books to Read 31

Index 32

Introduction

There are many different kinds of animals. All animals have babies. They take care of their babies in different ways.

These are the six main animal groups.

Mammal   Bird   Reptile

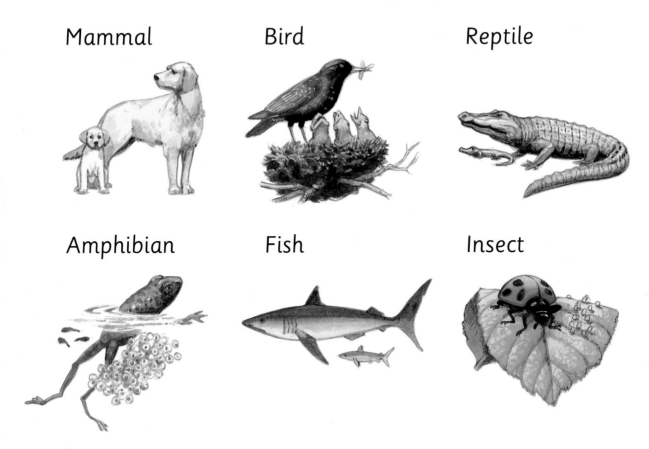

Amphibian   Fish   Insect

This book is about insects. There are more insects in the world than any other kind of animal. Most female insects **lay** eggs. The babies often look very different from their parents.

This is an adult fungus beetle next to its babies.

What Is an Insect?

All adult insects:
- have three parts to their bodies—head, thorax, and abdomen
- have six legs
- have two feelers called antennae

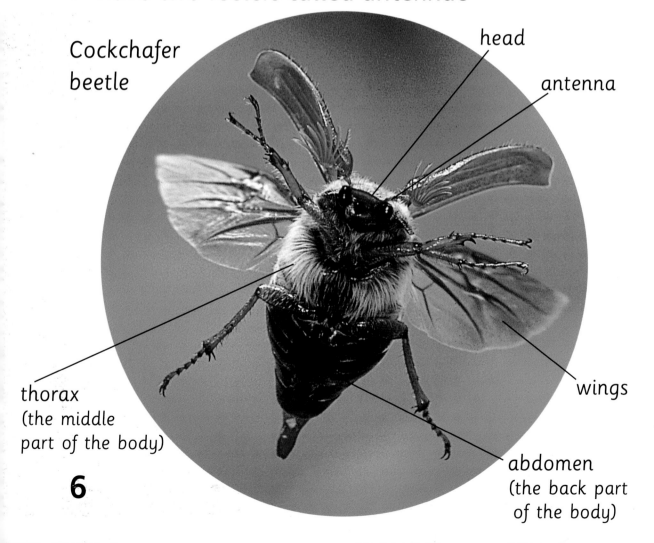

Cockchafer beetle

head

antenna

thorax
(the middle
part of the body)

wings

abdomen
(the back part
of the body)

6

Most insects:
- have two or four wings to help them fly
- **hatch** from eggs laid by females

When this giant atlas silk moth is at rest,
it leaves its four wings open.

Laying Eggs

Most insects **lay** their eggs near a plant or a dead animal, so that when their babies **hatch** they will have something to eat.

Baby flies are called **maggots**.

Some wasps sting a caterpillar or beetle and put it into a hole. Then they lay an egg in this hole, so their baby will have something to eat when it hatches.

This sand wasp is dragging a caterpillar to its **burrow** for its babies to eat.

Taking Care of the Eggs

Most insects do not take care of their eggs. Once they have **laid** them, they just fly away. A few insects do stay with their eggs and babies, **protecting** them from **predators**.

This female earwig takes care of her eggs.

Some insects, like ants, termites, and some bees and wasps, are different. Thousands of them live together in a **colony**. They take very good care of their eggs and babies.

Worker bees take care of the **queen** bee's eggs.

Hatching Eggs

When the eggs **hatch**, some kinds of insect babies look very different from their parents. These are called **larvae**. Many larvae eat their old egg cases.

These ladybug larvae do not look like their parents.

Other kinds of insect babies look more like their parents. These are called **nymphs**. The nymphs do not have wings. Some live under water.

This dragonfly nymph hatches and lives under water.

Finding Food

Nymphs and **larvae** are always hungry! Some eat huge amounts of leaves and fruit.

The larvae of butterflies and moths are called caterpillars.

Other young insects attack and eat other animals.
Many eat other insects.

This ant lion larvae digs a hole in the
sand and waits to attack passing ants
that fall in.

Taking Care of Baby

Most insects do not take care of their babies. They may even eat them! Insects that live in **colonies** do take care of their eggs and **larvae**.

These ants take care of their young in underground nests.

Insects that live in colonies often have a special room where they keep their eggs and babies. They bring their babies food to eat.

Worker honeybees bring their **grubs** food to eat.

Staying Hidden

Many animals feed on young insects. Some young insects try to stay hidden from their **predators**. They are often the same color as the plants they live on.

These Kentish glory moth caterpillars stay hidden by being the same color as the leaves they eat.

Some **nymphs** that live in water need to hide from hungry fish. They make a home out of pieces of plant and sand. They carry their homes around with them.

This caddis fly nymph is hard to see.

Staying Safe

Some insects have a horrible taste. They have very brightly colored skin that warns **predators** they taste bad.

Cinnabar moth caterpillars taste horrible to predators.

Another way insects keep from being eaten is to surprise their **predators**. Some insects try to make themselves look like a bigger animal to scare their enemies.

The black dots on this puss moth caterpillar look like big scary eyes.

Amazing Changes

As insect **larvae** grow, they get too big for their skin. Their old skin splits, and they climb out with new, bigger skin. This is called **shedding**.

This ladybug larva is shedding its skin.

The skin splits for the last time, leaving a **pupa**. Inside the pupa, the larva is changing. Soon the pupa splits open and the adult insect comes out.

This ladybug is crawling out of its pupa.

Splitting Skins

Nymphs do not turn into **pupa**. They already look a lot like adult insects. When they are big enough, they split their skins for the very last time.

This dragonfly nymph has climbed out of the water and is ready to **shed** its skin.

24

This adult dragonfly is climbing out of its nymph skin. Its wings look very crumpled, but they soon will grow big and strong.

The adult insect climbs out of the nymph skin. The new adult insect often stays very still while blood pumps around its new body.

Growing Up

This is how an insect **larva** grows up. The larva does not look like its parents.

Growth of a swallowtail butterfly

1 The adult female **lays** her eggs.

2 The larvae **hatch** from the eggs. Butterfly larvae are called caterpillars.

3 The caterpillars eat lots of leaves and fruit. They get bigger and bigger.

4 The caterpillar turns into a **pupa**.

5 A new adult butterfly crawls out of the pupa.

This is how an insect **nymph** grows up. The nymph looks a lot like its parents.

Growth of a grasshopper

1 The adult female lays her eggs in a hole in the sand.

2 The tiny nymphs hatch from the eggs.

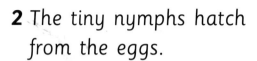

3 The nymphs eat all day. Soon they split their skins.

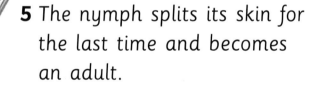

4 Each time they split their skins they get bigger.

5 The nymph splits its skin for the last time and becomes an adult.

Insects and Other Animals

		Fish
What they look like:	Bones inside body	all
	Number of legs	none
	Hair on body	none
	Scaly skin	most
	Wings	none
	Feathers	none
Where they live:	Live on land	none
	Live in water	all
How they are born:	Grow babies inside body	some
	Hatch from eggs	most
How babies get food:	Get milk from mother	none
	Parents bring food	none

Amphibians	Insects	Reptiles	Birds	Mammals
all	none	all	all	all
4 or none	6	4 or none	2	2 or 4
none	all	none	none	all
none	none	all	none	few
none	most	none	all	some
none	none	none	all	none
most	most	most	all	most
some	some	some	none	some
few	some	some	none	most
most	most	most	all	few
none	none	none	none	all
none	none	none	most	most

Glossary

burrow   hole that an animal makes in the ground to live or hide eggs in

colony   group of insects that live together

grub   type of larva

hatch   to be born from an egg

larva   (more than one are **larvae**) animal baby that hatches from an egg but looks different from an adult

lay   when an egg comes out of a female insect

maggot   baby fly

nymph   young insect that looks like an adult insect when it is born

predator   animal that hunts and kills other animals for food

protect   to keep safe

pupa   shell of skin that a larva grows inside

queen   mother insect

shed   to lose an old layer of skin when a new, bigger one has grown

worker   insect that does all the work in a colony, like building tunnels and feeding the babies

More Books to Read

Crewe, Sabrina. *The Bee*. Austin, Tex.: Raintree Steck-Vaughn Publishers,1997.

Himmelman, John. *A Ladybug's Life*. Danbury, Conn.: Children's Press, 1998.

Holmes, Kevin J. *Butterflies*. Mankato, Minn.: Capstone Press, Incorporated, 1998.

Theodorou, Rod, and Carole Telford. *Big & Small*. Crystal Lake, Ill.: Rigby Interactive Library, 1996.

Hartley, Karen, and Chris Macro. *Ant*. Des Plaines, Ill.: Heinemann Library, 1998.

—. *Mosquito*. Des Plaines, Ill.: Heinemann Library, 1998.

—. *Snail*. Des Plaines, Ill.: Heinemann Library, 1998.

Index

abdomen   6

animal groups   4, 28–29

antennae   6

colony   11, 16–17, 30

eggs   5, 7–12, 16–17, 26–27

food   8–9, 12, 14–15, 17, 26–27

grubs   17, 30

larvae   12, 14–17, 22–23, 26

nymphs   13–14, 19, 24–25, 27, 30

predators   10, 18, 20–21

pupa   23–24, 26, 30

skin   20, 22–24, 25, 27

thorax   6

wings   6–7, 13